west
of
west
indian

poetry

linzey corridon

MAWEN*Z*I
HOUSE

We acknowledge the support of the Canada Council for the Arts for our publishing program. We also acknowledge support from the Government of Ontario through the Ontario Arts Council, and the support of the Government of Canada through the Canada Book Fund.

Cover design by Peggy Stockdale
Cover image: TinoFotografie / abstract art portraying loneliness and hope or depression / Shutterstock

Faith Smith quote from "Queer Livity in the Caribbean: Rosamond S. King's Island Bodies." *Small Axe: A Caribbean Journal of Criticism*, vol. 21, no. 1, Mar. 2017, pp. 233–240.

Gayatri Gopinath quote from "Gayatri Gopinath on Queer Diaspora Aesthetics." *Imagine Otherwise*. 15 Aug 2018. https://ideasonfire.net/69-gayatri-gopinath/

Thomas Glave quote from *Our Caribbean: A Gathering of Lesbian and Gay Writing from the Antilles*. Duke UP, 2008.

Library and Archives Canada Cataloguing in Publication

Title: West of West Indian : poetry / Linzey Corridon.
Names: Corridon, Linzey, author.

Identifiers: Canadiana (print) 20240349199 | Canadiana (ebook) 20240349229 | ISBN 9781774151525 (softcover) | ISBN 9781774151532 (EPUB) | ISBN 9781774151549 (PDF)

Subjects: LCGFT: Poetry.
Classification: LCC PS8605.O7685 W47 2024 | DDC C811'.6—dc23

Printed and bound in Canada by Coach House Printing

Mawenzi House Publishers Ltd.
39 Woburn Avenue (B)
Toronto, Ontario M5M 1K5
Canada
www.mawenzihouse.com

For you, reader, loving and loved

And for Kevin, an island,
now and forever

Contents

Portraits *1*

Diary *27*

Musings *63*

Acknowledgements *103*

Portraits

What would these real lives give us, though? What do we want from the archive?

FAITH SMITH

Origins

There are no real words
only culpable emotions
funny bodies made into magic
pilgrims without (home)lands
our ancestor vagabonds
until now.

Here remain my people
the test of time eats away at them
my country in their hidden distinction
imagine boys shedding flair
envision girls between touch and gaze
they are my razed hopes and dreams
the woman who bands her breasts
smothering motherhood
the man living in the shanty
kicked to the curb by family
because water is thicker than blood
I claim you my kin
you endure simultaneous corporealities
my blood is the shade of you
the color of first kisses in the woods
when man-made shelter rejects your
claim to desire and to expression
the lone shopkeeper in the bus terminal
a public secret
the only role model many will ever know
I hold you between my hands, in my head
the islands writhing from the sweet
pain that is our continuance
the diaspora looks to you
bodies transformed into timepieces
maps into the land.

Amazona guildingii shriek for us,
and our half-written sinuous chapters,
they are to remain unfinished.
This is the tragedy of the Caribbean queer.

The vitality of the liberation movement is fleeting.
Fancies whisk away the next *He-She*,
the latest *Girl-Man* into disillusioned ecstasy.
Sociality sucks life out of tradition,

resuscitating *Bullers* everywhere
on the brink of suspicious predilections.
The procedure is a fluid one,
like rivers that partition us

into parcels of land to be occupied,
to be slashed and burned,
crafted from the image of the men
and women who till us thin.

Listen closely as the fluttering spirits sing
acknowledging our offerings.

Interview with a Chi Chi Man

So, where are you from?

                                        I was someone else

And what is your story?

                                          I was something pure

But when is your beginning?

                             I was one drop too little too much

Yet how did you get here?

                              I was the boy who rode the wind

                                   brisk, newfangled, unsettled

Then who will save you now?

                  I am the sea unending, rhythmic, fearless

                          I will save myself.

Pointa (Obeah Man)

White, perennial white robes haunt me
your head wrapped in blue silk excites me
how such a warm color provokes
the spirit to fear and awe escapes me
and my ability to comprehend
your seemingly human disposition
that which we share in common.

Perhaps my state of wonder
stems from the spirits accompanying you
around the village, through mournings,
weddings, baptisms, Sunday spirituals,
supernatural shields keeping the wretched at bay,
making space for the love of those men
who might decode the mysticism shrouding you
in power and privilege.

Such privilege is heavy.
How ostracizing one's life must be,
blessed with influence over the minds of men
yet stripped of your potential for earthly satisfaction.
How visceral your touch could've been,
no longer reserved for the one who gave you visions
free from the succor of rum, free from the burden
of tradition, free from the jumbie called culture.

I dream of your slow-dancing walks down the valley.
I still hear the spiritualists behind you
chanting the spells of a community
on the verge of extinction.

I observe a community clinging
to the diminishing life-force of an island
lost in time.

Tell me, Pointa
tell me what the ancestors sang in your sleep,
read to me from your shed fortified in galvanise
made to withstand a decaying coterie.
Who really was *the stain upon society*?

One thing remains certain.
No one wears the proverbial dress of fear,
love and admiration better than you,
Obeah man.

Xander

White house on skidded stone
octogenarian Xander endures alone
teenage boys looking to party
seeking refuge out of necessity
cold nights on their boat rides
down the Grenadines
high school boys alert yet tipsy
falling into the game for fun
risking death free from the sun.

Xander has no wedding ring and one key
meant for the room hidden from the sea
young boys dance across his poorly lit home
one, two, three, four
risking life and limb once more
old man serves drinks to the boys' galore
emboldened by every pour
young boys chant in ecstasy
their clothing loose and slippery
Xander leaves the key on the dresser
shuts the door and leaves forever.

Lorna

I.

To think that this warm woman
willingly left the hot and coveted south,
to find her destiny in the dry,
unforgiving air of a northern people and not mother nature,
nature just another body trapped under the feet
of Man's incessant penchant to manipulate
how beings are perceived, how mother nature
and West Indian woman ought to be understood.

So, she is in the North in pursuit of another,
the one who slipped away from her into the sky,
into the city, into freedom but not really
because freedom is a gun held against her head
she is compelled to freedom
she is to live and die by freedom
in pursuit of protection
the supposed comfort of Asylum.

II.

It's funny how asylum sounds like slum.
Slumming it in the ruins of the North
because asylum isn't really a ticket to freedom.
And besides freedom is a gun
Caribbean women carry in pursuit of love.
The gun is loaded and useless beyond feeling free,
it can't buy her a *poutine*, can't dress her in a warm coat,
it can't help her rob RBC to make rent.

Lorna and her lover are slumming it
with their freedom guns in tow.
These weapons obscure the scar from a beating
endured at the hands of her brother,
at the feet of her father,
the stone pelted by her mother,
wishing it would have killed her,
praying the fire caught her and her lover,
crossing their fingers and hope to die that
the plane falls into the sea,
cursing the gun against her head
that one day it will go *bang!*
But *bang!* must wait because winter always disrupts
the game of Russian roulette played out with freedom.

III.

Who wants to die at the hands of mother nature?
Not Lorna.
She is saving her death for the gun,
that piece of steel which she and her lover
unknowingly lost hold of the moment they jumped
onto the jumbo jet riding North to Asylum,
forsaking the liberty of controlling the gun
in exchange for the *come see me and be me*
world above the archipelago.

Come see me and come live with me,
two animals destined to rip each other apart.
Because freedom is a gun that is no longer in her control
and slum life eats away at them,
so does the comfort of Asylum devouring
(s)kin and muscle and bone and marrow
into nothingness.

Fatman

Gramoxone is for the pests
it also prevents *strong, raw,*
language from penetrating

the ones being pestered
what is an adopted mother
to make from toxic remains?

Nineteen times under the sun
a *shed* shielding you from the stars
a brother's belief your only light

This country's latest suicide victim
even in death we're robbed
of self-determination

I've saved this page for you.

Parner

Sometimes he sees without his eyes
that which the mirror reflects into the night,
into the Holocene of sea and stars,
the moment when he was still a small boy
who laughed, who kissed girls on their cheeks
and hid from the terror of happiness.
He'd kill to return there.

Maro

Potogey man,
in your stained capri shorts
reddened with history,
damp and heavy from violent encounters,
I watch you from behind metal bars.
How free you must feel
walking the streets of Yambou,
hastening on foot through Peruvian Vale
into Mesoptomaia,
through foreign villages and their bile.

Drunk from your latest affair
your face looks simple and
sombre from the bitter liquid,
or was it from the constant shaming,
dear *Buller man.*
You who spoke few words,
who always smiled at me in passing
as if to say *I know.*

You stay roaming,
drafting lists of other men
bursting from intoxication,
drowning their demons
and slitting love's throat
before it could ever articulate desire.

Maro, how happy were you?
your brown leather sandals
worn out against the pitch road,

the soles hinged to your feet
under the weight of your sorrow and joy,
redistributing the fat and the pain.

I wanted to tell you
that I am on a journey
in search of the times in which we live
I fail to make adequate use of
your memory now only a fantasy
conjured with your passing
an *accident* at home
a bullet to your head.

Did you flinch, Maro?
I close my eyes and picture
you and your guarded grace falling
at peace with imminent death
having encountered only the ugliness
of Man towards you.

Notes to My Husband

Black streams from you
yellows make up the sinew
of your blue heart
red liquid gushing from your lips
bright with the effervescence
of life
brown eyes cast a net
wide and white like your mind
a blur
one grand grey moment
in between golden suns
under the blanketed skies
footnotes
how I came to spend eternity
with you,
my *Batty man.*

Gold Teeth

We could have held hands through your storming,
your decadently destructive period of self-discovery
I could have caught those forecasted teardrops
if you would just stop shifting, Lagahoo,
we could have helped each other heal from the trauma
of sun and sand and sea and shame and secrecy.

What difference does all of this make
now you are in the big city,
in the hustle and bustle of forgetfulness
remember to drink three teaspoons of salt water daily
pickle your mind, your body, your legacy
and I will preserve you on this white page,
a Black man running from himself.

Pony Combs

Today marks one month,
your slipping away from the living,
leaving us behind in a cosmos of grief
we move forward
we know nothing else.

I remember the late-night call
your mum asked around for our number
she couldn't wait to let us know how much she
misses you, that you passed unwillingly,
that we needed to come pay our last respects.

Thirty-one days have come and gone
we speak of you, of the grief,
of the humor and the relief
Pregs seems tormented by it all.

We made it across the country,
pooling whatever little money we could gather,
making sure to buy your mum orchids, Pony
we were never able to deliver them
she stopped picking up the phone.

Pregs' sadness is my own
he speaks of dreams, of conversations,
the air is most suffocating on days
when we're awake
I love him the best I know how.

I close my eyes and return to the black sea,
a room filled with guests, enemies, family,
estranged lovers and foreign figures
the sermon was ravishing Pony,
whenever you could hear over the whispers,
the speculations as to the cause of death.

Spring is here in its depressing beauty
it rarely rains
perhaps your tears flow through Pregs
from his swamped existence
he is doing well
I am still with him.

I recall sitting on the bus on our way home,
holding Pregs' hand, trying to make sense of the grief,
wishing the air of scorn never made it to your side
I showered that morning, but I still felt grimy
they did you, they did our community dirty
I hope you covered your ears, Pony.
Dying is hard enough.

Summer arrives in another thirty-one days
and life flourishes then, I suppose
Pregs will be busier
his clay pieces less muddied
he moves forward with your memory
and I in tow.

We're still waiting for your mum's next call.

Blooming

Violets grow blue
in midst of you and your
tragic *mise à jour*
just as the islands are burning
faint traces of decayed desire
putrid like soured roses
sprout between your legs
your effervescence fades
in protest of pride's daisy facade.

Lilacs bleed yellow
under the weight of your sorrow
damp with the emotional
residue from your carbon flight
across a sea of flowers
up hillsides and down
the carnation path
bright green in anticipation
of your arrival home,
Funnyman.

Exulansis

Breathe.
When the villagers come for you
tell them you are not alone
sing to them our legacy
I am with you.

—History

Diary

What would it mean to live your life knowing that your life is radically bound up, intimately bound up, with those who seem so distant from you?

GAYATRI GOPINATH

Ritual

I am *here*
in communion with the seas
my life stems from cashee,
hard food, and bush tea, a feast
sugar and salt and pepper, this heart
a cacophony of soca and calypso
spawning from La Soufrière
I am a vessel bleeding fire
raging and treacherous and alive
I will not apologize
a library of visages precedes me
a forest of calloused hands awaits me
tread lightly, I a prism of trapdoors,
a haven rife with inexplicable opportunities
home is where the journey ends
I am ready.

Dear Caribbean

How can I appreciate you
from thousands of miles away?
the water between us is deep,
bitter with the salt called memory,
choking on macro and micro events
suffocating our future.

I remember when I was twelve
how you'd let me rest
my fat head on your tropic shoulder
how you would rest yours against mine
how in those moments we were one,
a breadfruit tree soon split into two
one branching north to die
the other remaining south as it withers.

These bitter truths come to me
in intervals, a white wave,
a blur inhibiting my vision
my body toxic from the bile
seeping out from these revelations.

I spit it all out into the eroding world
thousands of miles away
into the suffocating air,
into the warming void meant to make us
forget beginnings and endings,
our conception and extinction.

Brown Matter

Douglaa - (दुगला)
Caribbean Hindustani drifter
mixed-man branded *too much*
pretty boy with *two necks*
you made the *merchant* love the *slave*.

Bastard, you should be more grateful
illegitimate, you have everything
you will ever need
son of a whore, you cheated the Fates
into manifesting the inextinguishable truth.

Black Matter

My Blackness refuses to be defined
by the confines of Caribbean history
yet I am recognized as singular,
one-dimensional flesh and bone bursting
with symbolism in the story of North America
I remain abject
on the continent's iris, in the mis-gazing
perpetuated by the colonizer,
my Black is not up for debate
this voice is easily stolen
crushed under the knee of the settler's
obsession to control shifting narratives
I can no longer breathe
and yet I will continue to speak through
the shared struggle that is my experience,
the past of my partner's West Indian ancestors,
the present of my Black peers compels me
to reinvigorate my purpose, the future
of our unborn children demands that we shout
even in silence I will not be ignored
a knee on my neck will not be my legacy.

Quandary

A lifetime spent checking goals off a mental list
only to realize that
you set in motion a series of inevitable pit
falls
which come to swallow you whole:
REASON, CONFIDENCE, SELF-AWARENESS.

There's a science to the madness
the experiment recycles itself
you've become the guinea pig
your life now depends on factors internal,
external, trivial, essential, tangible, intangible,
legible, illegible:
CHAOS

utter CHAOS,
chaos injecting life into you
renewed with purpose
on a track you never anticipated.

I began a boy-child
I became something like a man,
monstrous
I remain that over which my people are divided,
the crudity my people half-hate
the sugar that sweetens lips at dinner tables,
the bitters that curb a nation's bellyache
I am seen, heard,
never both.

After the Travancore

The cosmos of curls atop your head
fails to resonate with the immigration officer
who ticks *Black* without your consent,
transporting your Indian grandmother's cheeks
elsewhere beyond the Canadian census,
her romance with a Black cane cutter rectified,
documentation of *what is* becomes *what should be*
paper, ink, policy hide a troublesome
history of love and lies deep and meandering.

You, sir, thought you'd be a pro at passing,
kicking, stirring, coursing through the globe,
a tinge of bronze permitting you to challenge
not having a single story.
What pilgrimage bestows lucidity,
a close proximity to light and sound?
You *lightskin-Black* mixed with the halo stolen
from your Douglaa mother and her battle for transcendence,
a war of worlds tearing her to pieces,
Gehenna consuming her head and Swarga Loka her heart.

To have a connection to Europe remains a curse,
the weight of civilization crushes you,
reality escapes your lips with every new sound
thick with the cadence of a conspicuous animal
stumbling across maps, living on precarity,
permitting your friends to threaten
your dead white sibling's memory with a single spell
but you don't look alike
what if we all resembled the binding of trees
our roots tense, prodded, interwoven?

When I die burn me four ways
once on Hairouna below La Soufrière
my second ceremony atop Mont Royal, Tiohtià:ke
take me to the degenerate seat of artificial life
and the Chamouni foothills to treat with whiteness
like terror once did, eviscerating the archipelago
long ago the Eastern Ocean shielded my foremothers
build me a pyre atop the sea and incinerate my remains
peer into the fiery abyss and witness
the indentured shaping new lands and people
after the story of the Travancore.

Ma

Sun,
progeny of a forgotten mother
his role is to be the man
she never had the luck of loving,
a man who cares unconditionally,
the stone that reinforces her labyrinth walls
a mere boy preordained homosexual,
meek bastion forever needed by one woman,
he exists to vindicate her,
Moon.

Dear Ma,

> All is well.
> I never write to you
> I refuse to worry you.
>
> Trapped in this cycle
> I've lost myself
> I've lost you
> our memories now misplaced.

> Help me,
> Your First.

He is unlikely to know Ma again

                                        they feel each other
                         past islands, across continents

She succeeded in raising him

                               lost in the sinister beauty
                    of paradise's heteromasculinities.

Ma, she who is everything
and nothing.
A rainsquall, a stormy sea, a hurricane,
a theory, a praxis, the body,
the melody made from wet feet against
river stones, hands tracing the wind,
the hymnal of island-nations
in the aftermath of organized chaos.

I am preoccupied with a longing
so ferocious, so transcendental,
a desire to escape self-imposed limbo,
my very present is a gift and
Ma remains a lifeline to the future-past.
I tote unrequited, ephemeral enigmas,
each one a brush stroke
coloring genealogical resistance.

In Memory of

all that persists
fighting for self-preservation
I bleed rainbows
leaving the living in awe
rattling the earth's core
speaking to the dead boy
who bent and bled for others.

He reeked of paradise that child
exuding the Caribbean sun,
he was black and frigid on the inside
in the shadow of beaches, flora-fauna,
sentenced to a sweet and simple life
that boy was trapped
to escape, I was to murder him.

Well trained in mutiny
I cut ties with the family
hacking away at generations
shattering ontologies
severing time-links to the archipelago
slitting the boy's throat thirty-six thousand feet
above the land for all to see.

Time's wound remains open
such precious colors within me
I stare at the kaleidoscope
my veins a mirror, reflections,
the rainbow hurries to my feet,
caressing my shadow,
swallowing the blackness,
a mosaic of jewel tones
reminding the boy of his false victory.

Passing Light

I want to know my father though
I can't imagine him beyond his father's obituary.
The faces I encounter beyond these two men
are colored by the labor of my mother,
and her mother before her,
and by my great-grandmother soothing
the fires of their busy-bodied lovers.

This patrilineal fire rages.
I feel it eating away at my core
yearning for more of the carnal,
but I am no ordinary man.
My fire burns from the fuel that is Junenia,
and Vera, and Estelle and the women of the Travancore
who left me their love in the form of muted words
roti, channa, Nani, karela.

How calm the women in my family must feel
gasping for air every time
the men in their lives looked away.
How thrilling these breaths are to take,
how exhilarating it is for me to share
this single draft of air with the goddesses
who watch over my pit as I journey
past my antecedents' watchmen,
willing a new universe into reality,
passing flames to hermaphrodite kin.

Illegitimate all of my life,

I am haunted by whispers of his greatness,
his deeds and his dreams; a life of treachery.

His existence means I must remain a fiction
in a place where nature makes and breaks futures.

Spreading his seed across the continents,
I've come to represent a passionate

afterthought, a pawn forged on a whim
when there was no room left on his game board.

Obituary: April 2020

A feeling of inadequacy festers
Sun, you choose to love a Black man
a failure circumventing father's expectation
daddy a *saga boy* by the archipelago's standards
his heart failed him for the fourth and final time.

> You've eaten the narrator
> now memory holds you hostage.

I guess you should've built another life
ensuring the family's inclinations remain strong
now all you have to offer your kin
is compassion and friendship and laughter
and companionship and security and a love so great
it created an island between pages.

My father was always just a memory
an unsolved mystery
I make home from his absence
I am swollen with loss
residue, unspoken words
the legacy of lives never embodied.

Concordia

There is power in the dead
their gaze looking back at you
from the page filled with emotion
as you safeguard mementos
keeping you bound to the living
though just barely.

You spend your empty existence
in ravenous search of communication
to other worlds
places where beings are set free
devoid of desire, of any cause,
rid of you
and your morbid fancies.

Frida Kahlo rejected the notion of surrealism

The 25th pharaonic dynasty was Nubian

Oscar Wilde went to church

He adored the opulence of Catholic rituals

The English Romantics were irrational

Gloriana never married

And so she died alone but a historical success.

History bombards you, *Buller man*
lost and full of self-awareness
you delve into books
breathing new life into history
in search of the magical pieces
to complete the community tapestry.

Plantation Ghosts

Marred, the eldest of kin teeters
atop the bloody order,
enduring consecutive catastrophes,
attempting to shield the youngest from peril.

With no armour of their own
the burden of the world crashes down,
crowning the skulls of those defenders
most in need of salvation.

Fate deals the veterans a fleshless existence,
garnering their hide,
a coat for the younger generations
who then hurry down the order to ruin.

I watched my sister from a distance
behind the screen of my iPhone
as she scooped up the remains of
her lover off the asphalt,
as she cupped his bloody, leaking head,
as she screamed for assistance from
onlookers who chose instead to film her

I witnessed the nation's hand retract
ever so quickly from her plea,
her palms stained with matter.
I was reminded of a time long ago,
a moment when the nation chose
to reject the notion of me
and my *funny*-boned comrades.

I stared at my computer
as time oozed from flesh,
witnessing her transcend naiveté
rushing towards despair,
as she came to realize
that she, too, could be made *funny*
under the watchful eye of plantation ghosts
steering our people away from one another.

Obituary: May 2020

My sister taught me strength
resilience
an unconditional love
given freely by children
unaware
how cruel the quotidian can be.
Dear world, I am so bitter
I will never forgive you
for taking her from me.

The island hoards memories
visions I can no longer parse
how to explain loss?
a feeling that is not a feeling
lives and longings once lucid
never material but *there*
tucked away in between
parietal and occipital lobes

I want to be transported
to the dreaming
that place of genealogies
and feasts and sadness
to be covered in a warmth
so threatening to the touch
weave me a blanket of respite

when my sister slipped away
I invaded the heavens
in search of the being
gatekeeping the temporal
but time is a beast
one I've always neglected
I still have nightmares to share.

Moon and Star

I hear accounts of your visits. Broken mirrors. Shrunken images.
It all feels foreign. You walking without feet. Ma sleeps with the
lights on. Your scent is everywhere. I believe she remains terrified.
You never return home. That all of the hurt she experienced from
you living audaciously, it would manifest once more.

Quebec

Montreal burns my visions to ash
into soot that covers me black
darker than the leather chelseas
carrying me through the West
through boyhood into confusehood
to adulthood and back to the ground
under my wooden soles

this terrible feeling on my skin is different
vibrations from my kicks stir the blackness
a frenzy of degenerating molecules
I hasten through the mist
on the warmest of snowy days
today I fail to conjure a life before the cold
the dancing wind absolves me of the tropics
on my never-ending journey to freedom

I speak for my skin, for the soot
moving in rhythm to the echoes of metal heels,
in praise of winter's penultimate vision
how can *les misérables* arrive at peace?
That is why I am on this journey,
for some peace in this horrible skin.
I am wrecked from walking alone
So, I've stopped moving
and now I wait for you to catch up to me
diaspora, my pseudo legacy.

Paris

The land of my birth refuses to love me back
pictures and videos of diaspora clutching their roots
dreaming of a place in which many will never live,
but they remain connected, they all haunt me

> *j'apprends cette nouvelle*
> *en transcendant le temps, le Louvre.*

How is it these taboo legacies misrecognize me,
leaving me outside the gates of our country's story?
The archipelago is fractured, repeating,
resonating half-truths and partial memories,
calling me *Buller man* every chance that it gets.

> I am reassured by these invocations
> across the Atlantic.

Greater Toronto Area

Every now and then I come
across a stranger on Lakeshore Boulevard,
into the tentative space of a passenger
on the number 35 Jane bus,
the gaze of the shop lady toiling away
at a storefront in the armpit of Ontario,
and I am compelled by the rhetorical
Are you West Indian?
Often the response is favorable,
sometimes I am met with gentle rebuke
no.

Cracks appear amidst my certainty
not because I am incorrect.
What I mean to say to the stranger is
I see my ancestors in you.
I feel a history swelling in their faces,
I hear a chorus of voices in their shadows,
I am comforted by the intention behind encounter.
And my inconsequential, *funny* life
is pulled and repelled by the ephemeral
legacies of distant worlds scattered in diaspora.

After all these years there has been so much
leaving, so much movement
I am descended from amphibious nomads
I move even when the earth stands still
sometimes it feels as though there is no axis,
no rhyme or reason to the revolutions I endure.

Leaving is never hard
return, now, you see, reader,
how to come back to a time,
to a place that has forgotten you?
There linger fragments,
traces of histories despite lapses

I never thought to leave,
to look back on muted departure,
certainty would be the chasm,
a black hole that sustains
the fickle parts within me
leaving brought with it surety

that one day I would arrive
gazing upon memories of a life
waiting quietly, a creature outstretched,
arms spanning time
in search of crystallized truths
no longer enough to hold me *out here.*

Two truths pursue me everywhere.
First, I come from a
mother, sister, father, lover
each of them islands.
Second, I am deathly afraid, terrified
that being *funny* will never be enough,
a chronicler in search of an audience.

I convey histories, acrid sermons,
for those who enter the world exposed,
transforming naysayers into believers.
May we dance with them,
may we dance with each other
on wretched grounds
as we learn to share the archipelago.

Musings

Who, through love and desire, loneliness and pleasure, were we hoping to be, imagining ourselves to be, and becoming through our many Antilles?

THOMAS GLAVE

Therapy

Dear self,
someday,
when you're happy,
try to forgive me,
try to forgive them.

Your people, your country,
your family, your memory
of the time that spat you out
in tattered pieces
try to love once more.

Remember
fear is a moment of artifice
an instance of parochial stasis and hesitancy
to embrace the potential for agency and power
to transform artifice into spectacle
alluring and devastating in the theatre that is your life.
You remain one in seven billion human beings
with seven billion billion billion atoms inside *you*
so just extend
perform.

Unmute

Bellow into the wind all weakness
rooted in the fears of an overbearing society,

the one that robs you of your femininity,
a country that drains you of your fierceness.

Let the current take with it
the burden of your ancestors,

a toll taxed with the memory of a nation
struggling to accept that which is sown into the land,

into the cane, into the coffee, into the cotton,
into the sweat dripping down the forehead

of your great-grandfather who tried to love a woman
in the hopes that he might outrun his queer transgressions.

Feel the air lift you pass the disquiet of your aunty,
the one who would visit Trinidad to indulge in her female friend,

the companion who never earned a name, a face,
her body bursting with affection of the flesh

for your aunty who preferred tank tops, and cargo shorts and flip flops
paired with alluring red lipstick and a full face of makeup,

aunty's own tiny rebellion against the unsympathetic
consciousness of a region denying her embeddedness.

You are in the sky now
between the earth and the stars,

free to write your own history of desire,
able to make love to your partner in all three spaces;

below the earth, above the sky,
between the stars as they ravage you,

as you delight in him,
as all five bodies devour each other.

We unmute history with every touch, every sigh, every tear,
paying homage to our decadent ancestry.

Will you sing?

Our life will have meaning
to many who suffer the same,
who live well and think good,
thoughts keen on small and kind deeds.

Our essence is what it should be
when we've turned to dust underground or at sea
with much uncertainty which is more peaceful,
though both mean serenity.

People will know about us,
the ones forgotten so mysteriously.
They will boast of our trials and our tribulations,
of our lovers and our enemies.

Our hope will rise from the ashes,
land on solid paper and transform
into the untold epic of our lives,
into the never-ending dream.

We scribble life and scatter
to Earth's corners,
every word having a soul purpose,
one task we leave to the future
beyond our passing dear orator,
chant meanings from this literature.

So, chant
ours is the bridge
keeping choruses
alive.

If you must sing our story,
what shapes would your mouth make?
what echoes resonate
from the darkest corners of this room
we call a world?
How sharp are the vowels
assaulting your vocal chords in protest,
in testimony?
Or will your consonants triumph,
the pining sounds rippling
upwards through the lungs,
flaring from your nostrils?

Perhaps your song is instead a hum?
Your throat vibrations buoying
memory under the moonlight.
If you insist on singing for the stars,
to stir up a longing
for many you'll never meet,
rest assured you have known
the *Batty man, Chi Chi Man, Anti* too.
You have only to remember
how to carry a tune.

The Shape of Love

Where I come from
the sea caresses fresh waters
it summons passageways
symbiosis
collecting our ugliest regrets and storing them
an endless record of the living
a constant reminder of the dead
the promise of togetherness for all eternity
this is a story both old and new.

They say we are trouble
(un)necessary problems.

I say to you
we are love
autarky and violence.

Where I come from
Funnymen self-select
free to self-immolate
a rum bottle in one hand
fractured desire in the other.

How easily misanthropes slip
into old ways
into belief that we couldn't see stars
even though many of us are ablaze
the pages of our lives lit up
Antiman now biblically secular.

It is always the powerful,
charged with recording melodies,
who write us wrong.
I am arranging a perpetual song,
one sustained by fortissimo bridges
and refrains syncretizing belief.

I am unlearning cycles
rhythms of silences and remembering
how to speak, how to smile, how to frown
how to be proud of the twist in my hips,
the glow of my skin in the shadows,
how the pressure of my voice echoes
into centuries past because of these words,
the miracle of becoming
embodied flesh and power.

I am unlearning love of the ugliest kind,
swapping stones and blades for empathy,
escaping the fire and brimstone into the sea
I ebb and flow like the morning tide,
caressing the shore, the land of my birth,
sopping the hands and feet of my persecutors
leaving them pruned,
making space in their *funny* toes and fingers for love.

I am learning to teach the broken about the damaged.

What if I am not
extraordinary?
How will you love me
then?
Will you cut across time
jaggedly
slicing your way through self-doubt?
Alien
I can see legacies more ordinary
simple
untraceable gestures signaling
breath.

I want you to tell me
how
will you love the untouchable?
Walk
in step with me and the moon
remember
astrology is a scam that nourishes
somewhere
we cannot see and touch and hold
home.

This love should feel like the afterlife
intangible
because *some of us don't come to stay
long*
the eons it will take to calm our village
unabashedly
make me float through the tears in space
rifts
you conjured with a single stroke.

Harm
there is blood leaking from your fingers
love
bloodshot, thick, and rusty
taste
can you smell it too, the iron?
Remember
you chose to forget me.

Alert the heavens
rupture my veins
I cannot forget to live
remember seven times
how to breathe
flood the cosmos
a palace atop my head
stargazing
mirror of a life (w)hole
a doorway to nowhere
there's something in me,
in the water, a cure
ornamental and obscure
schism-like, the ashes
now falling from above
do not love constellations
do not love me *without*
love me *with*
endure.

Research is Medicine

Teach Judith Butler about my struggles, Miss
Fanon might just write to you about my encounters
with potions and pyrotechnics, a philosophy of alchemy,
runes indebted to Wynter and her disassembly of monsters,
woman-wizard conjuring remedies atop oak
suspended somewhere between Cuba and Jamaica

ask C L R James how chemistry came to be in you
and me and in *The Palace of the Peacock*,
the one in which Caribbean people change skin,
endowing the Indies with earth and flesh and spit and shit
a cacophony of mystics swallowing up the Caribbean Ocean,
hoisting me up on their leathery shoulders,
transporting me to dungeon homes purple and thorny

like love in a Nalo Hopkinson dream,
my dancing with the brown girl is Glissant's natural poetics,
magnetizing inside and outside of the ring,
a breath on the wind that carries new wayward meaning
far away from the tragic vestibule, *you know*,
that place where epistemology once knocked boots

the river down the bayside still speaks of this melee
it burst the dam again, spilling onto the pages
of the clerk's blue ledger, a tattered horcrux
sending a tingle down my wedding finger
some kind of juju meant to remind me that yes,
magic realism isn't really real realism at all

Plascencia cuts a hole into pages of his people,
some kind of portal devoid of linearity
we slip into these portals and deduce treasure
a mountain of unbroken incantations longing for song.

The Shape of Contempt

There is so much rawness on the island. The people. The streets. The sea. Life teems. Restless and reckless abandon. We are. A swollen people. Grotesque mass of bile and anger. And sadness. Spilling over. Eviscerating everything. A people in a perpetually unrecognizable state.

A complicated story.

                                    A people cornered.

Africa-Europe-America.

                                    Our story is not.

Unique.

                                    The land bleeding.

Sorrow inherited.

Long sorrow bequeathed
belts
chains
tree branches
cable wires
umbrellas
shoes
pots and pans
big stones
misguided words

                            our chosen legacies.

A violence inflicted on the young.

                                        Our ancestors.
The colonial experience.
                              Rage continues to transform us.
A love of the ugliest kind.
                            We carry the brutal with us

              into adolescence,
            into the most passionate,
          uncertain years of our lives,
                              into romantic love.

At our core remains tension unresolved
an orbit of people and spectacles wedded to each other,
simultaneously diminished and augmented
impressions of suspended believers, a dissonant tribe
with shoddy limbs implanted firmly in Equuleus.

There is something becoming in dissonance
cognitive, musical, devastatingly human
some semblance of tomorrow lives in between
something and nothing, someone and no one,
here and nowhere, between forever and a day
an inkling of intention melded with curiosity
feeds the opaque, irreconcilable parts within us.

In Transition

There exists a place in between worlds
on planet Earth where we congregate
in constant limbo, condemned by the word
and by tongues festering with empty promises

Forbidden is he from open embrace.

Outside the reach of the book's influence
the forgotten thrive in ecstasy
their community blossoms for none to see
every human flower, bearing forbidden fruit

Forbidden is she to love for fear of disgrace.

They gather in the fringes outside the faith
watching faith's hellish grasp diminish
observing their own strength proliferate;
hope lies not on a leaf in archaic text

Forbidden is it to hope for a future.

Every generation brings them one step closer
to the promised land, to Mecca, Varanasi
every new life enjoys a greater taste of a common goal
and every old life falls short of that victory

Forbidden are they to dare to prosper.

In transition from outlaw to abject
every being reaches their true potential
every man, woman, and child discerns truth
life never discriminates, people do.

Donkey Say World No Level

Curses are inexorable in the eyes of the beholder
lost in thick, uneven folds crafted from the sea's sadness
here remain lasting emotions
mountain ranges soon to exhaust our bodies
made into paper porous and pious,
unflinching, our story bleeds
through its nostrils, through eyes and dissonant ears
we are what we are unable to see
stuck in between three generations forward,
three generations backward,
we are the seventh state,
the state we feel and the emotions we become.

Like lightning outside its bottle, we search
for conductors to ground us past promises
forged from love and light transformed into visions,
faint recollections of passivity and contentment
wash over us and link us to lore,
to the dawning of alien peoples whose only
difference is that they be recognized as nonnative
all messages of normalcy,
every exchange between hegemonies passes over
spaced heads and arrives at the root of those lasting
and endemic vessels of patience and fury,
kindness and madness, desperation and elation,
into the animals and into the trees
we have experienced so many lives and yet
we are but toddlers learning to wipe our noses.

West of West Indian

Never remember the colonizer
washing up on our shores
from galleons tainted with goods,
degenerative treasures, one pound
in exchange for generations.

That was long ago
yet we remain prisoners
the sterling sits atop our heads
as we continue to indulge in
self-destructive displays of culture
we islanders love culture, exude it,
must internalize all of it
the good, the bad, the ugly.

Let me tell you
in my transition
to another country,
another identity,
this culture,
the legacy willed to me
by my Douglaa mother,
by her Coolie mother,
by my white-man father and
legacy preceding him,
it has failed me every other time.

Let me tell you
what holds value in my next life
is that abject piece of me
cast out by paradise.
What saves me,
what will save you,
is unappealing currency
more than tired relations,
double standards,
and paltry promises.

Let me remind you that I, that you,
that we will never be extinguished.

Fe A-we

Inspired by Kamau Brathwaite's "Letter Sycorax"

So, what if we die?
we will disintegrate
and the land will be nourished
seeds will burst forth as weeds
hungry for sun, and air, and life,
the inhabitants of volcanic soil
free from civilization
as we nativize the Caribbean.

This…

This book is

This book is an offering

This book is an offering not

This book is an offering, not the first

This........is...................not.............................the last of its kind.

Acknowledgements

This book first took shape in a literary environment that fueled my creativity. Thank you to the city of Montreal and to Concordia University. To my friends and colleagues who engaged with early drafts of individual poems, you are forever a part of this work. Thank you to Krsytale Tremblay-Moll, Rhonda Chung, and to H Nigel Thomas for providing such wonderful feedback. Thank you to Idman Nur Omar, one of the work's greatest supporters and my most generous critic. I am indebted to you and to our extended phone calls.

My thanks to Mawenzi House for believing in the message behind this collection. Thank you to my editor, MG Vassanji, for both understanding and supporting my vision for this project. Thank you to Nurjehan Aziz for her continued commitment to bolstering voices from the margins. Thank you to Kaitlyn Csenkey for always making sure that the contents of this book circulate widely and frequently. Thank you to Peggy Stockdale for the cover design and Sabrina Pignataro for working on the book design.

Some of the poems included in this collection first appeared via different publication avenues. Thank you to the editors and publishers at *Intersect Antigua, Wasafiri, Headlight Anthology, Kola, House Anthology, Montreal Writes, Insight Journal*, and *Emotional Magazine*.

To my partner in life, Kevin, this book is no longer just a dream. Thank you for trusting in me. To my mother, thank you for continuing to grow with me throughout this creative process. Despite all our trials, we still walk together.

LINZEY CORRIDON is a mixed-race (Afro-Euro-Indo Caribbean) educator and Vincentian Canadian poet and critic. He is the 2021 recipient of Canada's Vanier Canada Graduate Scholarship and is currently completing doctoral work on the nuances of the Queeribbean quotidian at McMaster University. His writing has been published in *The Puritan, Kola, SX Salon, Hamilton Arts and Letters, Montreal Writes* and more. He lives in Hamilton, Ontario.